Narcissist

Inside the Mind of a Narcissist

Paul Sorensen

Paul Sorensen

Paul Sorensen

TABLE OF CONTENTS

Paul Sorensen

INTRODUCTION

You probably already know at least one narcissist. Heck, you might even be one yourself! Because the inability to recognize your own failings is so deeply ingrained in the condition, narcissism is very rarely recognized by the very people afflicted by it.

Think of your friend who everybody loves, who knows where to find the best of everything, and who got you into the best parties in college. They're great fun to be around, but there's something you can't put your finger on. Then you remember their short temper, and how when you broke up with your partner, they were concerned about what her would think of them for staying friends with you. It didn't occur to them to ask how you were faring.

Once you look past the party boy, the one for whom life is just effortlessly fabulous, you'll see the darker side.

Narcissism has become an increasingly popular term in pop culture, and is used to describe almost any behavior that could be slightly selfish. Unfortunately, this only serves to water down the real understanding of narcissism, and leave you without any true understanding of the condition, until one day, you meet a true narcissist and have to deal with the fallout.

This book will explore the history of narcissism, and how it is defined today, both in society and by professionals as a personality disorder. It looks at whether or not narcissists can change, and how you can protect yourself if you find yourself as a victim of the widely unheard of narcissistic rage – a phenomenon that can be scary at best and downright dangerous to your safety and even risk your life at worst.

So, read this book and learn how to identify the narcissists in your life, and how to protect yourself.

Studies show that narcissism is only on the rise, and shows no sign of abating. Learn how to manage the narcissist in your life, and perhaps ultimate change your life, and theirs.

Thanks, I hope you enjoy it!

CHAPTER 1

What is Narcissism?

Narcissism, in its simplest form, is excessive interest or egotistical admiration of yourself, both in physical and metal attributes. Someone who is a narcissist likely exaggerates their actual characteristics, and may be extremely arrogant. At the severe end of the spectrum is Narcissistic Personality Disorder, a recognized mental illness.

Narcissism is named after a hunter from Greek mythology, Narcissus. Know far and wide for being extremely handsome, Narcissus was the son of a river god and a nymph. Narcissus was exceptionally proud of his own looks and achievements. The myth goes that one day Narcissus was walking through the woods, when a nymph named Echo saw him, and fell immediately and deeply in love with Narcissus. She followed him, but Narcissus sensed someone there, and rejected her, telling her to leave him alone.

The nymph was heartbroken, and spent the rest of her days in lonely glens in the forest, until nothing remained but her own echo. Nemesis, who was the goddess of revenge, heard this story and decided Narcissus needed punishment. She lured Narcissus to a pool of water, where he saw his own reflection and fell in love with himself. There are multiple versions of the myth, but in most Narcissus eventually realizes that he cannot have the object of his affections, being himself, and commits suicide.

Everyone needs a little taste of narcissistic traits in their life, in the form of healthy self love. True narcissism however goes beyond this. Narcissists focus on multiple areas of their personality, and have multiple traits across these. A popular book from 2012, Narcissism: Behind the Mask, lists the following traits as evidence of narcissism:

- Obvious self-focus in exchanges with others
- Problems sustaining satisfying relationships with others
- Lack of awareness of their own disorder
- Difficultly with empathy
- Difficulty distinguishing self from others
- Vulnerability to feeling shame, rather than guilt
- Haughty body language

• Flattery towards people who affirm their inflated self worth

• Detesting those who do not admire them

• Using other people, with no consideration of the cost of their actions

• Pretending to be more important than they actually are

• Bragging and exaggerating of achievements

• Claiming to be an 'expert' in multiple fields

• Inability to view the world from other's perspectives

• Denial of both remorse and gratitude

The exact definition of Narcissistic Personality Disorder varies between experts, and there is currently no line in the sand as to when behavior crosses over from being egotistical to disordered. Generally, many consider the behaviors to be a problem only when they start to negatively impact upon the individual, and the people surrounding them. It's estimated that approximately one percent of the general population is affected by Narcissistic Personality Disorder.

Historically, narcissism was called megalomania. The concept has been recognized throughout history, but it is only relatively recently that narcissism has been defined as a recognized mental illness. In 1785, the play Narcissus: or the Self-Admirer was performed in

Paris. It wasn't until 1898 that the term was first used in a clinical setting. The English sexologist Havelock Ellis used the term narcissus-like to reference someone who has become his or her own sex object, using the term to refer to excessive masturbation. Paul Nacke, a psychiatrist and criminologist, first used the term narcissism in a study of sexual perversions.

It wasn't until the early twentieth century when narcissism started to be investigated from a psychological standpoint. A paper was first published in 1911 by Otto Rank, but the most famous paper was that of Sigmund Freud. Published in 1914, it was entirely on the topic of narcissism.

Although nearly everyone will have some narcissistic traits, high levels can manifest as the personality disorder described in modern times. Today, it is defined as someone who overestimates their abilities, and has an excessive need for affirmation and admiration. Narcissists tend to think they are better than everyone else; they may also have a lack of interest and ability to maintain caring relationships with others. They will often inflate their own intelligence or abilities, despite evidence to the contrary, and can be extremely selfish.

A little bit of narcissism may not be noticeable to the general population, but as someone progresses further up the spectrum, the narcissistic person can engage in behaviors that become harder and harder to ignore. They anger easily, can skip classes, work or obligations often, act in a highly sexualized nature, and can quickly turn from loving to unexplained acts of maliciousness and hurtfulness. These actions quickly undo any benefits the narcissist may achieve from initially being seen as outgoing and popular in the early stages or more subtle versions of the disorder.

There are multiple tests for Narcissistic Personality Disorder, the most widely used being the Narcissistic Personality Inventory. A forty item checklist is based on the clinical criteria from the DSM (a manual of mental illness and their classifications).

Interestingly, although the condition continued to be discussed right through the twentieth century, some say that a new age for narcissism is now dawning. Since the year 2000, test scores on narcissism psychological tests on US citizens have continued to rise each year. Are we becoming a more narcissistic country every year? Psychologists have linked the results to the rise of the social networking and online culture. Perhaps by the time the next hundred years has passed, narcissism will no longer be viewed as disordered.

CHAPTER 2

Identifying the Narcissist

We all have narcissistic personalities and tendencies to a degree. It's nearly impossible to live in the modern world without them. We are all trying to make our way in life in the same environment. Sometimes there will be disagreements and bumps, it happens. There are however certain people who want to demand our attention and praise far more than normal. They thrive from trying to be the 'big man on campus'. Everyone can be self-centered or selfish at times, but a narcissist will take it to a whole new level. They'll be the life of the party, the one always out for a good time, who knows where to get exactly what you need, whatever it is.

So, how do you identify a narcissist? Think of your group of friends – a narcissist will have a very high sense of self esteem and importance. They think they're more physically attractive than anyone else, perhaps they pause each time they pass a mirror. Perhaps you've heard the stories about how they're smarter than anyone else in their class at college, or at their job. Perhaps you have a friend who is happy to accept your congratulations when they talk about their many achievements, only to lash out if someone should outshine them.

Narcissists thrive in big groups and large cities. They love any field where they can take the lead, and where they can be in the spotlight. Narcissistic tendencies usually peak in the teen years, and then decline with age in regular people. Men are more likely to have strong narcissistic personalities, and many more men than women are diagnosed with Narcissistic Personality Disorder.

Narcissists are thrilled with any complement, and will strive to associate with their admirers. Research has found a strong correlation between narcissism and perceived physical attractiveness. Narcissists tend to be impeccably groomed and dressed.

However, narcissism also has a dark side. Research has shown that people scoring high on the narcissism scale can argue more than regular people, and use more sexually charged language, even in neutral situations. They want to be 'top dog' in any interaction or relationship, and their language and actions are all geared towards being the one with all the power in any interaction.

A study conducted on college students gave narcissistic participants electronically activated recorders, which they carried everywhere they went for four days. The participants did not know when they would be taped, so the could not engage in deliberate behavior when they knew there was someone listening in. Therefore, it's likely that the behavior witnessed during these four days was a real reflection of their actions. The study found that a number of social behaviors usually viewed as negative by the general population were common in interactions by the narcissistic volunteers.

When socializing with others, the narcissists were more likely to swear, argue or become enraged with their peers. They were also more likely to 'talk dirty'. Even after adjusting for words used in anger, narcissists used more sexually charged language in every day talk. Finally, they found that narcissists often dodged obligations or shirked duties, including academic requirements. The researchers don't believe that the study participants were lazy, but instead using their manipulative behavior to avoid becoming engaged in any way.

With this knowledge, and a little observation, you'll quickly recognize the narcissist. They'll be the one expending an incredible amount of energy making the entire group notice them, metaphorically shouting 'Look at me! Look at me!' over and over again. When you do talk to them, if you can get through their harem of adoring groupies, then it'll be all about them. You may be lucky enough to ask one question before hearing all about their latest conquest (at work or in love!) for the next hour. It's best to just stay out of a narcissists way, or better yet, find a new place to hang out.

So, how do you know when someone has crossed over from just having high self esteem into being narcissistic? In the current day and age, we're all told over and over again that we're amazing, and that we should love and cherish ourselves first and foremost. Rarely is any kind of self love talked about in a negative light. Stop and think for a moment, and ponder the person in your life who seems to have an abundance of self esteem and self satisfaction. Now, think about all the times you interact with that person. How do you feel when you think about dealing with this person? If you feel all warm and fuzzy and happy inside, then your friend is likely just one of those lucky people who value themselves and others equally. However, if instead you ever feel ashamed, confused or unappreciated, then it's time to stop and look again. It's highly likely that this person in your life is a narcissist. Narcissism can look so similar to high self esteem, but ironically is likely to have the opposite end result.

If you are wondering about a particular friend or associate, next time you talk to them, try asking them about their biggest challenge right now, or something they're working on changing. If they are not afflicted, then you will get a real and thought out response. Most people spend some time thinking on their flaws and wanting to improve their life. Narcissists on the other hand, will tell you that there's nothing about themselves they'd change. They believe that they are already a perfect work of art. Any imperfection is intolerable. Therefore, they will never try to improve themselves or broaden their experiences, and whatever criticism comes their way (and they are often their own harshest detractors) will be buried and denied. Narcissists are often trapped in the cycle of refusing to accept any imperfection in themselves, while simultaneously denying that their own self and behavior has anything to do with their unhappiness.

Narcissistic people will even go so far as to throw tantrums and suddenly anger should you suggest that there is anything wrong with themselves or their life.

Psychologists called it narcissistic rage – an explosive and unforeseen reaction to the suggestion that they might be anything less than perfect.

To understand narcissists, you must first realize that underneath it all, they likely detest themselves. They hold the external opinions of others to the highest regard, and constantly think about how society, and their immediate circle, perceives them. They believe that their entire self worth is built upon their meeting of these criteria. They become addicted to achieving status in society, and crave praise as an expression of love and acceptance. The problem then comes from the narcissist's inability to value all parts of their life and personality. What goes up must come down, and our lives are never all amazing or all disappointment. Healthy people learn to accept this, and even enjoy the rollercoaster of life. This is possible only when we have something we value in ourselves outside of oth- er's expectations or their valuation of ourselves. A narcissist is unable to do so, they cannot accept any- thing than perfection from themselves, and often also from the people surrounding them. They therefore face a constant struggle to maintain perfection in the facade the show the world.

So how do you deal with narcissists in your everyday life? Note, that these recommendations do not apply in romantic or extremely close relationships. These types of relationships require a special touch, and are discussed in their own chapter. These tips can help you cope with a narcissist in your life where they are not involved in a major part of your daily health and wellbeing.

Not all responses will suit every occasion, but by utilizing these techniques, it will make dealing with the narcissist in your life easier, and remove the frustration for you.

Firstly, if you can, behave how they expect you to. Decide that how you treat them is not a reflection on reality, and will not influence your true self. Then, place them at the centre of the decision if necessary, and stop trying to express your own ideas and feelings to them. Realize that doing so will get you nowhere and give up on trying.

That said, if a narcissist loses their temper with you, or intimidates you in any way, then don't ignore this. Stay calm, and push back. Explain that you will not tolerate being treated like this, and be assertive and dominant. If they whine, tell them to stop, but do not escalate the conflict. By asserting your own dominance, you will effectively stop their own dead in its tracks.

If you find yourself stuck in a situation you don't want to be in with a narcissist, the easiest way to bring them around to your point of view is to lay on the praise. Next time you want them to agree to something, try dropping a large dose of praise and reinforcement. You don't have to lie, just be general like "You know, that situation would allow you to show off your amazing potential in this new field" or "I bet the boss would really notice your superior knowledge if you presented the project next week."

If all else fails, simply refuse to engage. As soon as you get that prickling at the back of your neck, walk away. When it comes to dealing with a narcissist, you can either win the argument, or keep your sanity – pick one. The narcissist will soon learn that you refuse to engage with them in any way, and will likely pass you over as you refuse to reinforce their view that they are superior to yourself in every way.

CHAPTER 3

Narcissistic Personality Disorder

As discussed, we all have a little narcissism in us, and many people manage everyday life successfully, despite the condition. However, when taken to its extreme, narcissism becomes Narcissistic Personality Disorder. This is a disorder where the individual has an extremely inflated sense of their own importance and a deep desire for admiration and adoration. They are preoccupied with power and prestige to an extreme degree, and are unable to see the damage this is doing to their own lives, and to the lives of others they interact and are involved with.

People with Narcissistic Personality Disorder (NPD) are often described as self centered, cocky, demanding, and manipulative. Someone with NPD will likely be convinced that they deserve special treatment, and will act like it too. They will also likely engage in aggressive behavior, and risk-taking activities. Symptoms of NPD include:

- Reacting to criticism with anger or humiliation
- Taking advantage of others to reach their own goal
- Exaggeration of their own importance, talents and/or achievements
- Entertains unrealistic fantasies about gaining success, power, intelligence or romantic relationships
- Has an expectation of favorable treatment
- Expect others to simply go along with any of their ideas and plans
- Expressing dislike or disdain for those they find inferior to themselves
- Requires constant attention and adoration from others
- Becomes jealous easily, and believes that others are always jealous of themselves
- Pays little attention to the feelings of others, and pursues selfish goals
- While coming across as very tough-minded, can in fact be hurt easily

There are different theories on the causes of narcissism. Although most believe that genes play a heavy involvement, opinions differ on the environmental causes. Some believe that narcissism stems from neglect or abuse very early in life, while others believe that in fact the opposite, over-indulgence and un-abated praise, with few limits set by parents, is the more likely cause. Another school of thought is that narcissism itself does not develop until the teen years. Some think that narcissism peeks as teens, and mellows by middle age, while others still profess that narcissism will only get worse with age, as their grandiose plans fail to come to fruition and their physical attributes lessen as they naturally age.

Whatever the cause, narcissists live in a world where they cannot trust the outside environment and other people to meet their emotional needs. In their own minds, they are complete unto themselves, with no need for anything that someone else can give them.

Many confuse narcissism with very high self esteem, but there is an important and clear difference. NPD crosses over from healthy self esteem into self adora-tion. A narcissist puts themselves on a pedestal, and expects others will naturally recognize their bril-liance. Someone with a healthy high self esteem, while they will love themselves, does not value them-selves as more important than other people or above others in their life.

Narcissists have an inherit belief that they are due special treatment simply for who they are, and can become very angry, very quickly, when they are denied it. Often the other person will have no idea that how they acted has been perceived as a slight towards the narcissist.

When this happens, something called narcissistic rage can occur swiftly. The term was first used in 1972, by Heinz Kohut, and Austrian born American psychoanalyst who studied narcissism extensively. It was Sigmund Freud who first realized that narcissists felt an implied injury in the 1920's, and Kohut has expanded further on this condition.

Kohut believed that because of how a narcissist views their sense of self, their very self is being called into question with the perceived narcissistic injury. They are therefore prone to oversensitivity to any perceived slight towards themselves, resulting in narcissistic rage. They must react strongly so as to regain total control over their environment. They must both remove the other person's ability to harm them, while regaining control over the situation and rebuilding their inflated sense of self, to restore their own sense of safety and power. The narcissist may also feel a strong sense of shame over their 'failures' being called into the open, which may also result in the stronger reactions of narcissistic rage.

A perceived insult or threat towards the narcissist can lead them to feel extremely targeted or injured. When these symptoms of anger are expressed in return, they are called a narcissistic rage. Symptoms can range from relatively mild and non-violet, to an extreme outburst. They may range from simply ignoring the perceived injurer, or being mildly annoyed, through to full on, violent attacks.

More subtle reactions may also include the narcissist being visibly irritated, 'tisking' or shaking their head, or expressing vocal disagreement with the situation. A more severe rage can include outbursts of physical violence, both at objects and people, shouting and strong physical actions. You may have seen athletes who throw the bat across the field when they are called out, or know someone labeled a 'sore loser' – these are both examples of narcissist rage.

What's important to recognize with narcissistic rage is that it differs from true anger in that it is unwarranted, and often caused by a neutral event that a non-narcissist would struggle to even identify. Real anger is a natural response to an identified frustrating or annoying event, and will usually dissipate after the anger expressed. In opposition, a narcissist rage can blow significantly out of proportion, and continue well after the initial event. Some narcissists find themselves trapped in a cycle or rage that perpetuates itself, while others may only experience the occasional burst when in a perceived extreme scenario. It is also not unlikely to find the sudden burst of rage to be followed swiftly by the 'silent treatment', both of which are used as a method to punish the perceived offender.

If you find yourself faced with narcissistic rage, the first thing to remember is to not engage. You will never be able to 'win' the argument, or make the narcissist believe that you did not mean to offend them. If you react in any way, it will only serve to exacerbate their anger. Almost any response you give, sans agreeing with the narcissist, will fan the flames and could escalate the situation to physical violence. Even logic and reason will not help once the situation has escalated to this level, and nothing that you say or do can change the narcissist's beliefs at that moment.

If faced with a narcissistic rage, the best thing you can do is walk away and refuse to engage with that person, even at a later time. If you are unable to do this, there are several methods you can use to limit your risk and exposure.

First, establish your personal boundaries, how much you are willing to put up with. If you reach this threshold, then leave the room, or the house. They may follow you, but if you do this consistently, the narcissist will learn that you will not react to their rage attacks.

Learn how to keep yourself calm. If you cannot re-move yourself from the situation, then showing no reaction at all is also beneficial. Learn how to calm your breathing and anxiety and try to create a sense of detachment from the behavior. If you continually show no recognition or reaction to their anger, it will give you some control of the situation.

Following that, simply accept their point of view, just for that moment. Remember, that the rage is not about you, or anything real that you did. Whatever you say to justify your behavior will not be heard at this moment. Once the narcissistic person has calmed down at a later time, you can try to discuss the issues that lead you to the reaction in the first place.

So, what hope exists for both those diagnosed with NPD, and their loved ones? Although at first, narcis-sists may come across as very popular and charming, the long term social outcomes for those with NPD are not good. Long term relationships are difficult, as people become wise to their true natures, and on av-erage, general levels of narcissism drop dramatically by age 30 across the general population. When this happens, such behavior is deemed more and more unacceptable by their peers. If the narcissist continues as they grow older, they can find themselves ignored completely by their peers.

But, is it even possible for anyone to change their very personality? The cause of NPD is not widely agreed or understood. Like many personality disorders, the cause is thought to be a combination of genetics and environment. It's believed that genes may play a significant role, up to 50%. But, along with this, the unique experience of each person and their interactions with others influences whether an individual will develop narcissism, and to what degree. This includes a relatively new influx of cultural factors that encourage narcissism.

It's thought that individuals with NPD come from a background where being vulnerable was treated badly, or was seen as a defect. They fear being dependant on anyone else, for any reason. People affected with NPD have learnt to suppress and ignore any perceived incompetency or vulnerability and hide it under a mask of self importance and competence. It's not that people with this personality disorder cannot change at all, but that doing so threatens their very self, the image that they are perfect and can do no wrong. This lack of flexibility or willingness to change then creates failed relationships, which simply reinforces their original position.

To explain, you cannot be narcissistic alone. You need the adoration of fans and reinforcement of your superiority. As time goes on however, they have a moment of narcissistic rage, or they let something show they didn't meant to let slip, and the fear that they will be 'found out' grows, and you show less and less of your true self. The very same people the narcissist was trying to impress become alienated, and this convinces the person with NPD that they need to do better to hide their flaws next time, and so the cycle goes on.

Even if they should meet someone who seems to see beyond their mask, and could offer a more authentic relationship, most sufferers of NPD are convinced that this only means they will somehow eventually be deemed unworthy. This fear builds up, and unfortunately, this means that those closest to the narcissist will often be the ones who suffer the most projected anger and rages. The greatest irony of the condition is that the efforts narcissists put in place to protect their sense of self, are in the end the cause of the rejection that they fear so much.

The first stage of treating NPD then can become an effort to change the traditional relationship patterns that a narcissistic person relies on. To encourage them that they can be loved, warts and all, if they will let someone in. The wall of protection can then soften and eventually possibly give way to true intimacy and emotion. There is no cure for Narcissistic Personality Disorder, but with psychotherapy people can learn to relate and react to others in a more positive way. The goal of psychotherapy is to help the narcissistic person to develop better true self esteem and also more realistic expectations of others around them. If the case is severe, then medication may also treat the more serious symptoms.

Clinical diagnosis and treatment for NPD can be rare however, due to the narcissist's close held belief that they are something special, and the mere suggestion that there could be something with them that needs addressing can send them into a downward spiral. Information however shows that narcissists can learn to be more caring about others, which in turn reduces their own narcissistic tendencies as they participate in more social interactions.

However, new research from Wilfrid Laurier University has suggested that narcissism may be less complex that previous research suggests. The study suggests that rather than being a complex moral failing, narcissism may be simply a mechanical failure of the brain to mimic, something that comes so easily to most of us that we do not realize what we're doing.

Humans regularly use mimicry to inadvertently copy others in a social situation, for example taking a sip of your own drink when a person sitting opposite you does so. Professor Sukhvinder Obhi, who undertook the research, states that he believes that rather than this being innate, the ability to mimic is learned on an individual basis. He believes that this ability is what starts the bridge towards empathy and true understanding of others.

For a narcissist, who has not developed this ability, their understanding of appreciating what others are thinking is hampered by their lack of understanding and mirroring of others actions. The narcissist therefore takes a more basic, utilitarian view of others. They believe that narcissists do not mirror other's behavior and actions naturally, and this leads to them having real problems fitting in with social situations. By training this behavior, he believes that narcissism could be lessened.

CHAPTER 4

Relationships with Narcissists

Unless your partner is on the extreme end of the spectrum, narcissism can be hard to spot. Narcissism in a complex condition, and by looking only at the most glaring of problems, you can easily miss the more subtle aspects and features. Put simply, you may well be in a relationship with a narcissist and have no idea. Looking back, you can often see what you thought of regular behavior in a new light, particularly if your partner is male. The stereotypes of masculinity in our culture applaud many of the traits of narcissism, such as grand plans and stories and an extreme ego.

Narcissists engage in promiscuous behavior at higher levels than the general population, always looking for the next best thing. Research has even shown that the more committed a partner is, the more they look elsewhere. Therefore, it's imperative to know if you are in an intimate relationship with a narcissist.

Narcissists believe that they are always right, and if you disagree with them, then it's obvious to them that you therefore must be wrong. This can lead to your needs and desires feeling very neglected. You may even be made to feel silly, or incompetent. For a grown adult, this can be a very foreign feeling that can leave you without a way to deal with it upfront, or even recognize what's going on in the relationship. You may start to challenge your own long held beliefs, or start to think that you're actually the reason the relationship is having problems.

Do not expect the narcissistic partner to have any interest in your life, outside of how it reflects back on him. Never expect an apology, or for them to try and make amends, should something they say or do cause you distress or harm. A narcissist will never take responsibility for how their actions impact any part of your life.

Particularly if they see you as an authority figure, or you have something they want, a narcissist will flatter you to the extreme in the beginning. As long as you don't matter to their own sense of self worth, or you have some quality they think will reflect well on them, you will be treated very well, to the point it could be mistaken for true love. But, as soon as you try to get close to them in a real way, you will then become a possession in their mind, one that can be used as necessary to validate their own image. The sudden turn from decent treatment into being used, ignored, or outright anger and abuse, can be very difficult. It can take a long time to realize that the expression of your affections, that a normal person would be flattered by, is what can trigger the opposite in a narcissist.

Don't feel bad, or put yourself down, if you find yourself in a relationship with a narcissist. You didn't do anything wrong, or should have noticed something you didn't. In fact, at first attraction narcissists often have a lot going for them. They're well groomed and fashionably dressed, often charming and very smart, and people will tell you how much they've achieved and that they're a 'great catch'. A narcissist will let you know from the beginning how great a catch they are. The problem that many fail to recognize is that this puts you on the back step from the start of the relationship.

A good way to decide if you're being manipulated by a narcissist is to stop and examine your own behavior instead. Do you often find yourself wanting to do things for this person, that to anyone else, you would say no? Are you constantly walking on eggshells around them, worried that some small or unintentional action on your behalf will upset them? You may end up finding yourself in the bizarre situation of doing something you don't want to do, or may even be contrary to your own beliefs, simply to please the other person, but you can't put your finger on why.

Here's what to look for in a new or existing relationship.

1. Pushing feelings of insecurity. Narcissists genuinely feel they are better than anyone else. While someone with a different disorder may engage in the same behavior to play games, or to make you feel inferior, narcissists truly believe they are superior, and will use methods, subtle or otherwise, to continually reinforce this. Think of the colleague at work who always blames someone else for the project failing, when really it was their own decision, or the relative who's always late to the party but tells you that your invitation wasn't clear. Narcissists will often 'block out your light' so they shine brighter.

2. No Mr. Sensitive. Narcissists, for all their public posturing, are believed by many to be very insecure at their core. They don't like to talk about their feelings, particularly negative ones, as this can interrupt their internal narrative of superiority. Because they

lack any positive feelings and emotions for them-selves deep down, they are unable or unwilling to form genuine loving relationships with others. To really love someone else, you must first be able to love yourself.

3. Talk resolves around self. Narcissists love to talk about themselves, their achievements and accom-plishments. They will happily talk about how their day was for hours, but quickly lose interest when you try to reciprocate. When first meeting someone, pay attention to how much they talk about themselves, or try to work their own experiences into conversation regarding your own life.

4. High need for control. Narcissists desire control in every situation. They believe that they are the best person to handle any situation, and loathe to give control of anything they're involved in over to anoth-er person, be it a work project or a date. This may manifest as controlling behavior, such as the husband who gets angry when dinner isn't ready the instant he walks through the door. You and your actions are only as good as how well you meet their needs.

5. Loves attention, at all costs. Ever gone out with someone, only to find they spent more time flirting with the wait staff than talking to you? Narcissists

crave positive attention all the time, and will instigate any form of contact or communication to get it. They may flirt with someone else right next to you, or keep the lines of communication open with all their ex-partners. Underneath it all, they're saying to you 'See how much everyone wants me, you're lucky that it's you I chose to be with.'

6. Cannot handle criticism. Heaven forbid that you ever need to talk to them about a real problem, because narcissists cannot handle even the smallest criticism. Beneath that polished exterior can lie a deeply insecure person. Anything that might tarnish their self-made image of perfection, no matter how small, must be immediately and thoroughly discredited.

7. Refuses to admit fault. Going hand in hand with point 6 is this one. Narcissists will never admit they were wrong, about anything – ever. They will even deny that they ever committed the offending deed. A narcissist may also flip the situation on its head and try to convince you that no, you actually said that to my mother, not me. It's enough to make you think you're losing your mind. Forget ever getting a heart-felt apology – it's just not going to happen. While the argument may seem like nothing but a small disagreement to you, for a narcissist they are fighting for

their entire self worth. They will dig in and never give any ground, over the smallest thing.

8. Using you. Do you ever feel like your relationship is one of convenience? A narcissist will use you and your things whenever it suits their end goals. This includes your belongings, your money, and even yourself. If you're going for a night out and have taken the care to dress up, you'll be reminded how you must look good so everyone knows what a beautiful partner they have. They want you to know how good you have it, simply because they chose to be with you.

So, how do you handle a relationship with a narcissist? First, check to make sure the relationship is not abusive. Not all narcissists are abusive, but their personality traits can easily become abuse if not held in check. If you are facing an abusive relationship, and it doesn't matter what type of abuse, then you need to deal with that first. Whether it's emotional, physical or even financial abuse, a person's mental condition does not excuse it. Until your situation changes, the only action you should take is steps to keep yourself safe and remove the risk of further abuse.

If you're sure that your situation is safe, the first step is to try to get your partner to admit the problem.

We've all seen it before, the alcoholic who 'just needs a glass to relax'. Denial is the most well known of all defense mechanisms. Even if it's simply recognizing that their life or relationship isn't where they'd hoped it would be, admitting that there's something they'd like to change is the first step.

From there, your partner needs to want to change. However, beware any manipulation. If they cannot dissuade you, a narcissist may agree only to shut you up, before quickly moving onto something more to their liking. From there, try and assess how willing they are to change. Don't use going to therapy as a measure, many 'regular' people are just as leery of this. If your partner is simply willing to work with you to improve your relationship, then this is a step in the right direction.

From there, rather than telling your partner all that they're doing wrong, approach the conversation from a different angle. Instead, tell them how you feel when they talk down to you, or that you worry that you're not enough for them in the relationship. Multiple studies have shown that if you can express the underlying feelings behind anger, you have a far greater chance of healing and reconciliation.

Once you have expressed to them how you'd like the relationship to work, make sure you remind them when they slip back into old habits. Where previously, you might have brushed off or ignored a comment that made you unhappy, rather than start an argument, now you need to remember to call these behaviors into question, each and every time they happen. Withdrawing from the relationship will be negative in the long term, and will allow your partner to also fall back into their old habits, instead of listening to you and remembering your feelings evoked from their actions.

Finally, you may need to realize that you have done everything you can. If you've tried expressing yourself and your feelings, and listened to what your partner has said in response, and there is still no change, then there may be nothing more you can do. It may be time to sit yourself down and really think about the relationship. Are you staying because you really want to be there, or because you simply feel too invested to leave? Even if your partner says they're trying to change, little or no real world result can still end up damaging your self esteem beyond repair. No matter what the reason, no one deserves to be treated badly and put down over and over again. Unfortunately, regardless of the reason, if your loved one cannot change their own behaviors, then you may need to change yours and leave the relationship, for your own sanity.

CHAPTER 5

Female Narcissists

The vast majority of people diagnosed with Narcissist Personality Disorder are male, some estimates put them as high as 75% of overall sufferers of the condition. That's not to say however that women are not afflicted just as seriously. Women can certainly be extremely narcissistic, and can also suffer from Narcissistic Personality Disorder. There is an importance difference however, between female and male narcissism. Male narcissists tend to emphasis their success in pursuits of power, intellect, strength, money and social status – all things traditionally highly valued by men.

Females narcissists, on the other hand, tend to define themselves more on the success of their family and household, how well behaved their children are, and the success of their husband's career. Where a male narcissist may wear a perfectly tailored suit, female narcissists tend to ramp up their sexuality and flaunt their physical femininity. To this end, a female narcissist may often also suffer from an eating disorder, in their panicked desire to be perfect. Rarely do male narcissists have this same problem, though many will place importance on being extremely 'buff' and fit.

Interestingly, studies have found that a narcissistic woman, regardless of her underlying personality, is still more likely to socialize with peers than a narcissistic man.

A female narcissist will usually be over confident as to their attractiveness. Research has shown that narcissists are generally no better looking than the rest of the population, but a female narcissist will place extreme attention on makeup, hair and styling. Ever known someone who can't leave the house without full hair and makeup, even to just go to the letterbox? She will only wear the best brand names, and frequently purchases new outfits and accessories. A female narcissist is also more likely to undergo plastic surgery than her counterparts, the most common surgery being breast enlargement.

A female narcissist will see family and children as an extension of how well she is doing as a mother. Therefore, she may be incredibly judgmental of the parenting skills of the other parent, and even more so of babysitters or daycare providers. Nobody will ever be as qualified to look after her babies than herself. Her partner may find himself undermined with parenting decisions he makes, even in front of the children or others. She may setup very rigid rules that she insists you follow for the good of the family, but not stick to the rules herself, changing the game as she goes along. Unlike most women, who may hesitate to physically attack a larger male, when narcissistic rage overtakes a female narcissist, she will lash out as equally as a male narcissist would.

It is likely that the difference between male and female narcissists is simply an amplification of society's traditional expectations of both genders. Narcissists are extremely sensitive of their public image, and how they are perceived by those around them, and so they are transformed into the stereotypical archetype of what society believes the perfect man or woman should be.

Along these lines, narcissistic women who find themselves single in their thirties and forties, likely due to their personality tendencies, will blame their potential partners. They are not strong enough to handle a feisty, independent and strong minded woman who knows what she wants out of life. They're too intimidating. How often have we heard that very phrase in popular women's magazines?

However, along the lines of societal gender beliefs, studies have shown that female narcissists are actually far more likely to seek treatment for the condition, and accept help from a professional. Male narcissists are not only less likely to go to therapy if the opportunity is there, they are also less likely to admit they have a problem at all, let alone ask for the help.

What must be remembered at the end is that everything in a narcissist's life is carefully planned and arranged to reflect back onto them. A female narcissist insists that her children and well dressed and perfectly behaved because that is what society so often deems a mother to be judged on.

As with any relationship with a narcissist, there are ways to distance yourself, either from the behavior or the narcissist yourself if possible. When you have children together, this can become more difficult. You may have heard the saying 'Happy Wife, Happy Life'. By employing some of the management techniques discussed in earlier chapters, you may be able to still have a relationship with a narcissistic woman, but like any other relationship with a narcissist, you have to be willing to forgo your own needs continuously, which many simply find too much to bear for a lifetime.

CHAPTER 6

Dealing with the Fallout

Most often, when narcissism is discussed, it's done so with how to understand and deal with the narcissistic person. Very little advice is usually given to help the person who is feeding the condition. This person can often suffer tremendously from criticism and abuse from the narcissistic person, and may often blame themselves for the situation. Just like the narcissist, they can have a warped view of the situation, but unlike narcissists, will blame themselves for the other's behavior.

Narcissists are constantly on the lookout for someone who will reflect back to them their inflated sense of self worth. This has also been referred to as anti-codependency. Rather than simply enjoying the company of others, the narcissist is always looking for reassurance and adoration from external sources. Their own success is measured by their perfection, and the more people fawn over them, the more their ideal self is reinforced.

Along with this, narcissists can be extreme perfection-ists, and always demand the best, from both them-selves and others. This can manifest in a requirement for their friends and family to also be 'perfect', so to reflect their own perfection. In the narcissist's mind, everything and everyone is essentially reduced to an object. Some features or objects, such as a wealthy partner or a very good looking best friend, work to feed their feelings of self worth. On the flip side, if you are going through a tough time yourself, you may reflect as a failure to your narcissistic loved one, and suffer the consequences. So, how you can break the cycle?

Firstly, analyse how you behave yourself around this person. Take a breath and then think about your last two or three interactions. Did you pay more attention to their own needs than your own? Perhaps you let them talk endlessly to you about their latest promo-tion at work. Did you allow them to chose everything, and control the situation, or did you have legitimate input into how your time together was spent?

Narcissists can be extremely loving at times, seeking to have that extreme love reflected back to them. You may not even realize that you are being lead to cer-tain decisions, or being tricked into believing you have some trait or skill that is invaluable to the narcissist. Unfortunately, sooner or later, you will fail them and suddenly be found to be 'not good enough'. This is because, no matter who you are, you will never be able to completely fill their need for praise and adoration. You may find yourself going from the adored person of their dreams, to being found wanting and unacceptable quickly, and the change can be difficult to understand.

Sooner or later, in their never ending quest to prove their self worth, both to themselves and others, new acquisitions are necessary for the narcissist. As well as belongings, this can mean attracting the attentions of new people, to constantly reinforce that they are worthy and also seen as a 'catch' to the next new thing. Particularly at times of stress and problems in work or with the family, the narcissist can become obsessed with finding someone new to validate that he is worth something. If you have ceased playing your allotted role, perhaps due to stress or life problems of your own, it becomes extremely easy for the narcissist to cast you aside and replace you with someone he ranks more highly. Do not take this personally. It is not a rational decision, but instead comes from a reflection of what he deems to be his own weaknesses. In a way, this may be good news for you, as although it can hurt, unlike some other personality disorders, once the narcissist has separated themselves from you, often callously, you will usually be left alone.

However, if you chose to withdraw yourself, be prepared for the narcissist to suddenly start trying to 'woo' you again. The sudden lack of your adoration can be devastating to their own sense of self worth. If you move on, they will lose the validation that they received from you, and they then may try to make themselves the center of your life. They may devalue your own accomplishments and put you down, or go as far to attempt to block any efforts to form new relationships, solidifying in their mind that you are only valuable when serving to reflect their superiority.

To manage this behavior, remember that narcissism is a deep rooted disorder. None of the narcissist's actions or comments reflects on your true self. The only way they value themselves is through others, even through superficial connections. Being cruel or challenging to a narcissists will only serve to make them lash out at you, in an attempt to maintain the status quo. The best way to handle extracting yourself from a narcissistic relationship is to slowly distance yourself, without being openly mean or clearly avoiding them. Simply spend less and less time with them, and find new contacts away from the relationship. Realize that when you reach the threshold when you no longer validate their self worth, or they find your 'replacement', that they may suddenly ignore you themselves, so that you are not shocked when this happens.

Once you have moved on, be careful not to fall into the same cycle of pleasing others. It can take some time after you leave a narcissistic relationship, especially a close one, to be OK with regular interactions again. This is OK, and will become easier over time.

CHAPTER 7

Society Indulges

Narcissism is on the rise. In this new world of social networking and instant information and gratification, 'look at me' has become the new catch-phrase. The next generation, children born between 1982 and 1999, originally called the Millennials, are now often referred to as Generation Me. How has the now constant public exposure of our lives affected our personal relationships? From the now mass acceptance of Botox and plastic surgery, to kids sports that give everyone a 'participation trophy', we are becoming a society where the praise of all is tantamount. We are constantly pressured to keep up with the Joneses, but often forget that we are comparing our entire life to what is simply someone else's highlights reel.

More and more, we as a society are being criticized for the relatively new culture of encouraging self esteem, where feelings of high self worth are considered to breed success, rather than something felt as a result of achievements. We now need to invite entire classes to birthday parties, hover over children in the playground, lest they hurt themselves or someone says something mean to them, and we are even sometimes told that we are ruining our child's college chances if they are not sent to the right preschool.

In 2006, a study of 37,000 college students was undertaken to evaluate the impact of narcissism in current culture. Published as The Narcissism Epidemic, the study found that narcissism in youth has grown at alarming rates. In 1982, only 15% of college students garnered high scores on the Narcissistic Personality Disorder test. By 2006, that number had risen to 25%. In the 1950's, only 12% agreed with the statement 'I am an important person'. By the 1980's, 80% agreed. In 1967, 45% of US students surveyed agreed that 'being well off is an important life goal'. By 2004 a staggering 74% felt this way. Further studies by the same authors have found a weaker work ethic and a greater reliance on leisure time by the same generation, along with an increase in their singular pronoun usage (I, me), coupled with a decrease in their use of the plural form (we, us).

It is estimated that the rate of narcissism in twenty-something's is as high at 10%, and growing. Researchers think that by the time people currently in their 20's are 65, more than 25% of them will have developed Narcissistic Personality Disorder. Remember, the estimated percentage of the general population to have NPD now is 1%.

Some researchers believe that the rise is in part because there is far less pressure to display social graces and polite behavior in the modern world, as there has been in the past. Children are far more indulged, and some would say discipline has gone out the window. The relatively modern 'self esteem movement' has produced a generation of children where everyone gets a trophy just for participating. Alarmingly, studies have shown that 30% of students now believe they should get good grades if they simply manage to come to every class. Some believe that grade inflation is now a major problem at colleges across the country.

Many children no longer hear the old 'because I said so' and instead are reasoned with and take part in the decision making of parents in the home. Many small children are no longer given time alone to invent games or play on their own. Instead, most are enrolled in at least one after school activity, usually more. It's not uncommon to find children with a structured activity to attend every afternoon, all geared towards developing 'essential' skills the child will need to get into a good school, get a college scholarship, and excel at life. America wants to breed an entire generation of super achieving children, and the competition has instead lead us to create an entire generation of narcissists.

During the 1970's and 80's, the US became obsessed with celebrity, to the point that you can now be famous simply for being famous. Take reality TV as an example. It first started in the 1980's with The Real World, but exploded in the 1990's with Survivor. Now, however, there are multiple shows where the whole premise is around watching other people in their everyday lives. They don't even have to be placed in extreme situations anymore for us to watch. Reality TV promotes the most ordinary, and often dysfunctional people as special and unique, and tells us all that we must follow their every move with fascination.

Critics of reality television claim that these shows make celebrities out of generally untalented 'regular' people, and glamorize materialism, and fame itself. Think of the Paris Hilton sex tape scandal. The airtime given to the leaked sex tape with her boyfriend was, at the time, mind boggling. Now, it would probably be posted on Facebook and nobody would think it even slightly unusual. She is the perfect example of someone who has risen to fame not for her talents or deeds, but instead for inherited wealth and a controversial lifestyle. Paris Hilton currently earns over $10 million ever year just from sales of endorsed products – a staggering amount really when you stop and think about it.

Speaking of social media, many believe that it is responsible for the rise in narcissistic behavior of today. Social media encourages us to share every facet of our life, and create online profiles that highlight our achievements and stress how special we are. For example, on Facebook, the more interactions our posts have, the more they are shown to those who interact with us, creating an environment where we are left striving to be more and more amazing, unique, and controversial, so that those who we have marked as 'friends' (likely to include tens or even hundreds of people we have never met) will be shown our posts and reply in turn. Rather than seeing self affirming techniques of the digital age such as 'liking' posts or posting sexy pouting pictures of yourself as forging connections, many view these behaviors as instead creating a disconnect and an isolation from the individual and the real world.

Some researchers believe that the phenomenon starts in childhood. We are all aware of attitudes such as every child getting a participation award, or putting a prize in every layer of pass the parcel – let alone that now it seems to be expected that the birthday child wins the prize in the middle! Researchers now believe that it goes further than that. The My American Doll company has a line where you can custom order a doll that literally looks just like your child. You can even buy matching outfits for you and your doll in their online store. The website associated with the dolls is called innerstarU.com.

There is a book available through major retailers called My Beautiful Mommy. Written by a plastic surgeon, it's purpose is to explain to children why their mother is undergoing plastic surgery. The cover shows an extremely thin woman, dressed all in pink, with her (tiny) tummy showing due to her cropped shirt outfit. She is surrounded by star bursts and shimmering fairy trails, while her daughter looks on in clear delight, her arms thrown open wide to hug her mother. The blurb states "You and your child will follow along as Mommy goes through her plastic surgery experience and learn how the entire family pitches in to help Mommy achieve her beautiful results." Inside the book, the doctor is drawn with an almost comically small head, but extremely broad shoulders and visible pecs. His female assistant is blonde. When mother returns after her surgery has been completed and her bandages are removed, the small child compares her to a butterfly, saying her cocoon (bandages) have now been removed, and comments to her mother that 'you're the most beautiful butterfly in the whole world'.

Children's parties, once simple affairs at home, now regularly include the hiring of full size jumping castles, and legions of entertainment. You can even hire fake paparazzi to follow you around, pretending that you're famous. Baby's clothing ranges now heavily feature onsies with terms such as 'supermodel' and 'chick magnet' splashed across the front, and no one bats an eyelid.

Where once you would have been in big trouble at home for getting in trouble at school, parents now swoop in to rescue their child. School teachers and principals are regularly almost abused by parents, demanding that detention slips or bad grades be revised. In fact, the bad grade itself is often blamed on the teacher, rather than the student. All this can leave the Generation Me student without the basic skills to cope with personal consequences from their actions and without interpersonal skills to deal with anything other than utter praise and reflection of their own perfection.

While each could be seen individually as a random group of trends, taken together some researchers argue that it displays a shift in the modern day psyche. The focus of success is now on material wealth and a perfect physical appearance. Standards now suck otherwise everyday people into a world of McMansions with granite bench tops and after school pro golf lessons for six year olds. A popular song declares that "I believe that the world should revolve around me!" and nobody thinks this is a little odd.

The problem with narcissism becoming so pervasive is that many are self diagnosing, or using the word without understanding it's true meaning. Narcissism has become the new buzzword for magazine advise columnists and pop culture psychology. Politician and former presidential candidate John Edwards blamed his affair on believing that he was special and his becoming 'increasingly egocentric and narcissistic'. When the term is bandied about by popular culture, real conditions linked to it, such as Narcissistic Personality Disorder, can become misunderstood or watered down in understanding of severity.

Properly understanding narcissism, and how it is affecting modern day culture and the next generation, is crucial because of the possible long term consequences for society. The trend of 'fake it till you make it' is becoming an increasing problem, with fake riches (until the housing bubble finally burst), fake athletic achievements (Lance Armstrong, anyone?), fake high academic achievers (grading on a curve), fake friends (judging by the hundreds of friends on people's profiles on Facebook), and fake celebrity (YouTube and social media). While it all feels good, eventually, just as the mortgage crisis, it will come crashing down.

Ironically, much of our behaviors that many believe have created the so-called narcissism epidemic were started as an attempt to fix problems with low self esteem. Behaviors such as lack of caring for others, shallow values, self degradation, and aggression were all things that we believed boosting a child's self esteem would fix. Instead, it seems that it may have created a generation of narcissists, who exhibit this very behavior in spades.

In the long run, many believe that without forming real and healthy human relationships through empathy and understanding, ultimately we will be unable to avoid destructive behavior towards each other. Through empathy and understanding of how our actions affect others, humans have built a system that allows us to literally survive. As the story of Narcissus illustrates, without others we cannot survive. In the words of the great story, "Was ever …anyone more fatally in love? And do you remember anyone who ever thus pined away. It both pleases me and I see it; but what I see and what pleases me, yet I cannot obtain…we are kept asunder by a little water".

CONCLUSION

Thanks again for reading this book!

The important takeaway throughout this book is that narcissism is a condition that develops over an entire lifetime, and the reactions and treatment of you by the narcissist in your life has nothing at all to do with you, or indeed anything to do with reality.

If you're doing well and take the advice herein to heart, you may be able to admit that they have a problem, or that they may even need to accept professional help, but you cannot change them any more than you can change tomorrow's weather, and a loved one with Narcissistic Personality Disorder can be just as unpredictable.

It's also important that we recognize the direction that our society is currently heading in, and decide whether we should take steps, both as an individual and a greater population, to reverse the current narcissistic trend. Imagine living in a world where everyone acts like a reality TV participant – ALL the time. I'm not here to make friends, I'm here to win! What would happen to society then? Many think that the USA in particular has been sliding into a era of self obsession for a very long time.

Narcissism is, at its core, a very lonely and vulnerable place to be. It is only by forming long term and genuine connections with others that we can hope to reverse the trend. So, next time you're out with friends, or going somewhere new for the first time, stop taking photos of your food and posting it on Facebook, stop checking in on Four Square and take your time to look up and genuinely enjoy the company you find yourself in.

You never know, you might like what you see.

Thank you,

Paul Sorensen

PS. If you enjoyed this book, please help me out by kindly leaving a review!

CPSIA information can be obtained
at www.ICGtesting.com
Printed in the USA
LVHW020430170323
741781LV00033B/992

9 781502 320353